Unravelling

DANCING IN THE ETERNAL NOW

Ayesha Grant

Unravelling

A collection of poems written by Ayesha Grant

Dedication

I dedicate this book to my inner child.

Everyday, I am making all of your dreams come true.

- *Contents* -

Preface

For as long as I can remember, I wanted to write and publish my own books but a lack of confidence led me to create a series of roadblocks for myself. I always felt too insignificant to share my creations publicly. Too small. Too afraid of not being good enough, afraid that I would fall flat on my face. Afraid to dive into the non-physical nature of my dreams and pull them into the physical realm.

For a long time, I downplayed my gifts and lived in the shadows. It seemed safer there. It was comfortable. I had become accustomed to not being seen, so living like this became normal. So for a very long time, this was familiar territory to me and it became my home. It became a place that I could retreat back to, whenever the external world become too overwhelming or difficult to deal with.

I have noticed that this is a common theme among creatives. Even though they may be in possession of a brilliant idea or skill that should be shared with the world and celebrated, they choose to hide themselves away and quite often fail to see how amazing they are. But my awareness of the divine domino effect, filled me with faith and courage as I continued to believe in myself and breathe life into this book. This creation of mine felt incredibly sacred, so I was guided to not tell anyone what I was doing. As I continued to complete each chapter, it felt as though I was wrapping up a very special gift. Each page, representing another layer of wrapping paper. Another layer of myself. I felt compelled to handle this creation with care, as I protected it and ensured that it safely made its way through the cosmic birth canal and manifested into physical form.

Writing this book has served as a constant reminder that one can make a meaningful contribution to this world by simply showing up as their authentic self. This is always enough, it is enough to simply just be you.

There are times when life calls for us to courageously leap out of our comfort zones and dive into new territory in order to bring much needed change into our lives. This creates an inevitable domino effect, which gives birth to waves that ripple throughout the cosmos. Weaving in and out of different timelines like a cosmic tornado. When this happens, something shifts. It may be subtle or much more noticeable but either way, the shift has occurred. As a result of this, somewhere something has completely changed.

Every choice that we make has an impact on not only our internal realm but also the external, holographic reality that we reside in. As within so without. Everything affects everything. Someway, somehow. So a person who makes the choice to bravely jump out of their comfort zone is helping someone else, somewhere in the universe. Energy travels far and wide. Therefore everything that we do, whether great or small has an impact on someone or something else. To me, it very much seems as though we are simultaneously living out a number of different lifetimes in this one life. For those of us who choose the path of devotion, surrender and self-realisation; there tends to be a painful transformation process. This is followed by a series of metaphorical deaths and the release of the dense aspects of the self. An old part of us dies and gets burned away in the fire to be purified. Sometimes we barely have enough time to collect our thoughts before we are called to step into the next cycle and get ready to embrace this new version of ourselves that we have just given birth to.

The grieving process often takes place at the same time as this, which can cause a great deal of confusion. Nevertheless, this stage is very important; as of course it is to be expected that one would naturally mourn the part of themselves that has just died.

It is often painful to accept that we may no longer resonate with an aspect of ourselves that we were once clinging onto for dear life. But this is typically what the path of devotion looks like. It is filled with constant change and the need to adapt to new circumstances rather quickly. It is an endless rollercoaster of one death after another. Sometimes in the literal sense, as we may have to witness the death of those that are close to us, in the same timeframe that we our going through our own painful process of metaphorical death. This certainly intensifies the experience. But typically, having to ride a very large wave, tends to bring forth the opportunity to ultimately be catapulted further along on our spiritual path. I believe that whatever one find themselves dealing with, is exactly what they are equipped to deal with in this lifetime.

The unknown can seem truly frightening when you are standing on the other side of the bridge, looking at the life that you desire from afar. But once you take that first step towards that which you wish to bring to fruition, it becomes a little less scary.

Writing this book has taught me that great things do happen once you let go of the old reality that is standing in the way of those beautiful dreams that are patiently waiting to be experienced.

For a long time, I felt as though there were so many obstacles in front of me. It seemed like just as I was making progress, there was yet another hurdle that I needed to jump over. So of course, I would often go through periods of feeling completely deflated and tired at a soul level. It was only when I chose to go deeper into understanding the meaning of this human experience, that I realised how common it is for one to deliberately orchestrate difficult situations in an effort to learn the necessary lessons that will lead to growth. There are a number of other reasons why one may do this from time to time but ultimately it is happening to make the witness pay attention. Sometimes, this may happen because the individual needs to take action and make changes in a particular area of their life. For this reason, I am truly grateful for all that has taken place and everything that my experiences have taught me. The good, the bad and the ugly. It's all spiritual, so I must give thanks.

As my journey progressed, I realised that the only obstacles in my way were the obstacles that my mind had created. There was never an external enemy. The only enemy was the one within. The voice of self doubt, shame and guilt. The internal voice that said I couldn't publish a book yet because I didn't have a large enough following on social media, the voice that said *what if nobody buys my book?,* the voice that said: *perhaps my writing isn't good enough yet to publish?* All of those voices were aspects of my shadow. They were all different faces of the only enemy that truly exists. The part of the self that is afraid of being free.

From the moment we are born, we grow up being constantly told *what* to do, what *not* to do, *what* to think, *how* to think, *what* to eat, *when* to eat. This creates a protective bubble around the individual and often stifles free thought and creative expression to an extent. So there is often a lot to release and work through once one arrives at a place where they begin to remember what their own voice sounds like. There is truly so much to unravel as one becomes fascinated with peeling back the layers of their own being and remembering the supreme self that is silently dwells within the physical vessel.

Divine orchestration is always at play in this elaborately designed pantomime. So wherever you are, is exactly where you need to be. The Creator truly makes no mistakes but when we become attached to the physical plane, we are often not be able to see the deeper meaning behind our profound existence. Instead we continue to run into brick walls, until we finally surrender to what is and accept that everything is as it should be. Time and time again, the creator has reminded me of the importance of surrender and radical acceptance. Thus enabling me to eventually see that everything is and always has been, in perfect harmony with the specific path that the soul has chosen.

Acceptance and surrender, have been prominent themes in my life and this has allowed me to really understand the deeper meaning behind these divine states of being. Once I accepted that I had been a co-creator in all that had taken place in my life, I found myself draped in a newfound sense of freedom. It covered me completely, like a warm blanket. I felt extremely liberated and I found myself both excited and eager to create something that resonated with me at a soul level. I no longer wanted to participate in anything that did not feel meaningful to me. I no longer wanted to spend any time engaging in activities that did not contribute to the evolution of my soul. It was only when I took accountability for what I had chosen to experience, that I finally realised the power was in my hands all along. Ultimately, I was the one who had the power to change my circumstances and create the life that I wanted for myself. But I needed the contrast of being in places that did not resonate with my soul or feel good, in order to know what I *did* want my life to look like and what kinds of experiences I *did* want to have.

As I continued to make sense of this human experience, I experienced moments where I had the awareness that absolutely anything was possible. In these moments I felt limitless. In this place, there were no restrictions.

All along, there was nothing holding me back but myself. This was a hard pill to swallow but at the same time, it was very refreshing to bathe in such truth. The path was clear and free of debris, it was just me. Me and my inner twin within. Me and my beloved inner flame shining bright. So bright, that it could illuminate even the darkest night. I was unravelling and everything was unfolding in the most beautiful way. I am honestly not sure that words would be able to do the feeling justice. But it was a feeling like no other, realising that I had the power and that this was something that had been within me the whole time. This realisation made me feel completely and utterly divine.

Every single event that had taken place up until this very point, makes the most perfect sense. So sacred and divinely orchestrated, a life path perfectly crafted just for me. The supreme self within, was always able to see the bigger picture. Even in the darkest, coldest, loneliest moments. Perhaps this is why I have always been able to see the good in all situations. Particularly those that shattered my heart into a thousand pieces and broke it wide open. I have found that there are occasions where the pain is so utterly unbearable, that it tears the heart open and instantly brings the physical vessel to a humble state of non-negotiable surrender. These are precious moments, as they bring forth opportunities to lean into the abyss that is the timeless, elusive, untouchable soul.

Long before I was consciously engaging in shadow work or alchemy, I was constantly dying and giving birth to myself. Time and time again. I seemed to go through endless waves of radical transformation, as I surrendered to every metaphorical death that tightly wrapped itself around me like a coiled snake. Each time birthing a greater and more courageous version of myself. I was always so passionate about becoming the best version of myself and understanding why I am the way I am. Dissecting and making sense of all aspects of the self and my life was always high on my agenda and I continued to receive more clarity on this matter, as I dove deeper into my mystical soul. Countless hours in the

darkness, brought me into the light and slowly brought me back home to myself. Where I was able to blossom into the beautiful flower that I always knew I could be.

Whatever your dream is, whatever you wish to bring to fruition - it *can* be done. You are so powerful. More powerful than you realise and at any given moment, you can choose to remember your greatness and step into a more desirable timeline, if that is what you feel called to do. Everything is interconnected and there is truly no separation. Separation is the greatest illusion. Thoughts become things and we begin to witness the magic, once we remember that our words create realms.

In every moment, we are creating. Either consciously or unconsciously. Each and every thought that we put out into the cosmos goes somewhere. It does not just simply just disappear. It contributes to our reality in some way, shape or form. The universe is always listening. But the beautiful thing about life, is that there are infinite pathways available for us to take and any one of these can lead us back home to ourselves, eventually. The only difference, is that some routes may take longer than others and naturally, each one will possess a different set of chapters within it to be experienced.

This beautiful book came to life in the most natural way possible. It required no effort in the conventional way. This book was born, once I came to the realisation that my entire life was poetry. Everything that I did in my everyday life was poetry. Everything I spoke was poetry. It was a way of life, an expression of the love that flowed through my beating heart. I was always creating, always dreaming and always metaphorically dancing. My inner realm has always been a colourful and ethereal place. So ultimately, this book wrote itself. I was just the vessel that was used to bring it to life in the physical. All I had to do was step out of the way and allow the energy to move through me. Once the awareness of this washed over me, everything seemed to flow.

With the pen in my hand, I sat in my favourite little cafe on the beautiful island of Bali and the words just danced onto the page. It was truly magical. Everything just flowed. This made the process of creating the book even more special and due to this, I enjoyed every part of the process. I was in no rush to get the book published because I wanted to bathe in the sweetness of every moment of the creative process. Initially, this was a shock to me, as I had always been so impatient growing up. I always found the process of waiting so tedious and irritating but gradually something changed. I was changing. I was maturing. I was learning to trust the process of life, more than ever before. It's like waiting at a red traffic light. You know that the light will turn green eventually, so there is nothing to become frantic about. Slowly, slowly - everything always gets done. There is a time to stop and a time to go. A time to plant seeds and a time to enjoy the fruits of ones labour.

Truly accepting this, helped me to shift my perspective on the timeline of the various events that had played out in my life and the reasons why sometimes, there is a lengthy waiting process that one must adhere to.

For so long, I was lost in the wilderness. I frantically wondered what my life purpose was and tried so hard to make sense of the meaning of my existence and purpose for being on Earth. But that was the very problem. I was forcing, rather than flowing. Therefore anything that I was doing from this fear-based state of mind was not completely authentic or natural. Ultimately, this type of behaviour was not serving my highest good. As a result of this, for a long time it felt like I was pushing a boulder up a very steep hill.

I believe that when one is dancing to the unique song of the soul, there is an effortless state of flow that is experienced. Everything feels natural in that space and time ceases to exist. Suddenly, everything begins to feel like endless play, rather than hard and burdensome work. Of course, there will be times when one is required to overcome certain situations and put in some extra time or effort. But on the whole, there is a sense of calm and a sense of feeling supported when one hands their worries over to the divine and surrenders deeply to the cosmic embrace of the ever-present eternal soul.

So I invite you to come on a journey with me, as I unravel. Page by page. With each poem, more and more layers are delicately being peeled back, in the softest way possible.

Read each poem with an open heart and let the words come alive, as they create the most elaborate visuals in your mind. Surrender to the poetry, as these carefully chosen words transport you to a place that goes far beyond space or time. Welcome to the mysterious, sacred space that is my mind.

- Part One -

Lost in Paradise

Unravelling

Unravel with me

meet me in the astral plane and travel with me.

Don't be afraid to fly,

take my hand and we can soar the skies.

Look into my soul

gaze deep into my eyes,

this moment is eternal and the stars have aligned.

Tell me

can you see your reflection?

Do you see the divinity in this heart to heart connection?

Let's get lost in the eternal now,

dance with me and don't make a sound

because this moment feels truly sacred and profound.

Alchemy

All I know is intensity

so I want you to meet me beneath the surface where there's less density.

Heat me up and decompose me

let's get to this chemistry,

this is the first stage of alchemy.

I'm just a multidimensional goddess, shifting between dimensions

downloading codes and exploring the universe during astral projection.

Collapsing timelines and seeing the divine order in every connection.

I see the divinity in my own reflection

and the meaning of my existence is no longer beyond my comprehension.

Truly grateful to feel so at home in the abyss

because knowing my shadow so well, makes my power much easier to harness. Knowledge of self, is such a big part of this.

It's crazy to think that there was a time when I didn't even want to exist

now here I am, reciting this.

The ultimate plot twist.

Blossoming

With each breath I take

I can feel my divinity pulsating through my veins.

My very existence has become the perfect embodiment of art in motion

unfolding organically in live time,

unravelling oh so delicately.

A precious flower that is beginning to grow and take shape

I am blossoming in the most beautiful way.

Reflection

I look in the mirror and all I see is God

a masterpiece crafted to perfection with absolutely no faults,

everything is exactly as it should be.

The perfect avatar for this cosmically divine movie of mine.

The more I relax into my heart space,

the more I am able to see the magic.

I can hardly believe my eyes, I am in awe with the beauty of it all.

I am love and I exude love

therefore I see love in all things.

Divine reflections of me are all around

in every place, in every sound

this existence of mine is so profound.

With every breath I take

I am creating art.

With every step I take,

I am delving deeper into my heart.

Divine Union

This dance is so divine

existing far beyond the paradigm of time.

It goes on and on,

it feels as though I am dancing to my favourite song.

Every step that I take is in perfect harmony with the gentle whispers of
the universe.

All of the love that continues to flow to me, is exactly what I deserve

how truly amazing it is to finally see that I do deserve to be heard.

All I had to do was turn down the volume of the external world and turn
up to this party as myself.

Beauty is Her Name

For the first time, I could see myself

and what a beautiful sight it was.

The true embodiment of a Queen

So divine, so supreme.

Effortlessly giving life to all things, while dancing unapologetically
without fear.

I am exactly where I am supposed to be

I am home, I feel free.

For a long time, I could not accept the divinity that was naturally seated
within me.

The thought of it was just too overwhelming to bear,

so I chose to detach from the truth.

I made myself small and gave my power away

but I am happy to say, that is no longer the case.

At last, I have found the magical key that was so deeply hidden within
me.

I am no longer afraid to be myself.

It is safe to creatively express myself in all ways

At last, the beautiful journey home is gaining momentum.

No Words

Are there even any words for this?

I look around and all I see are divine reflections of me

everything is merging into one, right before my eyes.

There is no separation,

the walls around me are dancing to the rhythm of my heartbeat.

I sink deeper into the moment and I can feel myself getting lost in the
vortex of the great unknown

but I am not afraid,

fear is the greatest illusion and I refuse to participate in that old game.

It's over, it's done

I am becoming.

Into the Rabbit Hole

As I look into your eyes and gaze deep into your soul,

I see a love that reflects my own.

To fall deeper in love with you, is to fall deeper in love with myself.

I manifested the most divine mirror

a love so deep, a love beyond words.

This is like a psychedelic trip

and in every passing moment, I can feel myself getting closer to the peak.

I wonder how deep we can go?

If you are ready to elevate to the next level, just let me know and we can float.

Together we create thousands of new galaxies,

we give birth to realms that haven't even been thought of yet.

Dive into this new timeline with me,

follow the sound of my heartbeat as we take flight.

The magic will be revealed as we continue to breathe in sync,

tune into my frequency and the rest will unfold effortlessly.

A Whole New World

I am floating and I don't want to come down.

This place is so new, so fresh. I am so high above the ground.

What a relief it is, that I chose to go my own way and not follow the crowd.

In this timeline, it is safe to be different. Safe to be seen.

No more hiding, it's time to stop running.

I have run into myself at full speed, so many times

and every single mirror showed me exactly what I needed to see.

One of my clearest mirrors showed me that I was more powerful than I initially believed,

the reflection almost knocked me off my feet.

All I wanted to do was retreat back into solitude

my very first instinct was to run, fast.

Was this reflection really me?

I gazed deep into my beloved mirror

and suddenly I saw all that I needed to see. I saw me

To truly see you, is to see me.

To see me, is to witness divinity.

This Now Moment

Let's dance until the lights go out

because you my love, are a masterpiece that i'd love to mount.

I could stare at you forever and still not fully understand how our puzzle pieces fit so well together,

this is divine orchestration.

I know this meeting is somehow a part of my initiation,

so take my hand and let's dive deep beneath the surface

and if we drown, you will discover why I am so worthy of this crown.

I see the God in me, so I see the God in you,

you and I are royalty and I know that you feel it too.

A connection so divine, transcending far beyond the realm of space or time.

So I know you will never forget me, just as I won't forget you.

Perhaps we will meet again in another life

but until then, dance with me in this everlasting moment.

This moment is all we have, this moment is all that truly matters.

Epiphany

I see why they stare. This type of energy is rare.

For me, diving beneath the surface has always been a compulsory affair.

The deepest levels of surrender are required in this mystical timeline of mine.

There is truly nowhere else for me to be but right here,

it is not possible for me to run anywhere. Not anymore.

I can only melt deeper into this divine love.

The Dance Between Her and Him

I only know how to live authentically from the heart,

so meet me at the party and be sure to take off your mask.

Now that the initial union has taken place, it's time for us to dance.

Cosmic foreplay at its finest

I promise you, there is a very fine art to this.

Sink deeper into the present moment with me,

let's just take our time, there's no need rush.

It is important that we can can dance in perfect harmony,

all flow and no force.

Take my hand and dance with me all night long

as we become one with this never-ending celestial song.

This is like the most exclusive private party,

it takes place in public for all to see

Yet it is so private. So sacred. So dear to you and me.

Love

I want to experience a love like no other.

Divine. Cosmic. Something truly beyond words,

real love.

Deep, ethereal, holy, perfect divine-mirror type of love.

Not for the faint-hearted. Raw, authentic, deeply transformative.

Healing love.

A deeply sacred union that feels like a gift from above.

Unconditional love.

Love that goes beyond the surface,

truly in a category of its own. So unique,

yet something that i'd instantly recognise

A love that pierces through my tender heart and lights up the celestial skies.

Meet Me in the Eternal Now

Meet me in the eternal now

dance with me without talking. There's no need to make a sound.

With every step that we take, our hearts are beating in sync. Can you feel it?

Do you feel what is taking place right now, between you and me?

Effortless communication, non-stop flow.

This right here, is the purest form of telepathy.

I look deep into your eyes and instantly, you are somebody that I recognise.

I am home. You are home.

Two whole and complete beings rising in love, high on love. I would die for this love.

We had to ride one hell of a tide to get to this love, I cracked my heart open wide for this love. I would give up everything I own for this love, I found my true home in this love.

Being devoted to the divine, is a path that fits like a glove

and I must say,

I really do love, this love.

Take a deep breath sweet soul, it is time for us to take our rightful seat at the cosmic throne.

We have been apart for so long but we were never alone

we were always together, there was no separation.

How could anything be separate when everything is love?

This whole process is divinely orchestrated,

the most wonderful masterpiece has been created.

But before we could reunite, we had to come into union with ourselves and initiate the divine dance between the Sun and the Moon

allowing them to merge harmoniously, creating a cosmic explosion of love.

Once this was done, we would return home to ourselves

and after that, we would be able to see the divine dance in all things around us. We would finally know what is real, what is true.

Ultimately, to see me, is to see you.

To know me, is to know you.

This love is deeper than the undiscovered parts of the ocean but it is not possible for us to drown

because within ourselves, a home has already been found.

We are not trying to complete one another

rather, we are pure vessels of love

allowing all things to flow through us, including one another.

We are two hollow bamboos,

fearlessly surrendered to the present moment, exuding nothing but love. Gracefully dancing to the music that sprinkles down from the sky above.

03:03am

I no longer know what or where the comfort zone is, I am so far away from that place.

It only exists now as a distant memory,

a place I used to know.

Because in order to grow, the comfort zone had to be left behind,

I had to expand my mind.

Stage one, was thinking outside of the box

and stage two, was removing the box altogether.

If there is no spoon, then there is no box.

No limitations exist, besides the ones that the mind creates.

Everything is Art

Falling in love with myself again and it feels so good

I am worth it, I deserve this.

Every day is another opportunity to celebrate myself,

so every day is a special occasion.

Life is the most precious gift

but when it comes to navigating through every turn and twist, there is most definitely an art to this.

The key is to master it.

Gratitude

Thank you for showing me you.

Thank you for always being true.

Thank you for this mirror reflection of me, that I saw within you.

My greatest teacher.

One day we shall meet again, dear friend.

The face may change but the beauty that resides in the heart, will forever remain.

I will always recognise you.

Showing up, is all you ever need to do.

- Part Two -

Floating

Lost in Love

Look deep into my eyes, let's just forget about everything else for a while.

The background noise is irrelevant. Nothing else matters,

it's just you and I.

We fit together so well and we don't even have to try

and being in your presence makes me feel so high.

You are like a drug

and when we are together, I feel like I can fly.

Soul to Soul

I'm not yours and you're not mine

yet somehow, our paths are so intimately intertwined.

We found a home in one another and it was truly divine

but this connection was always so much bigger than you and I.

Our souls reincarnated here on Earth to make a change and set fire to
the old way,

we can no longer expand in the box of that old game.

We are here to embody love in all that we do

and it is important that we fully embrace this sacred mission and see it
through.

We must walk the righteous path and continue to spread our light

because we are no longer endlessly drowning in the abyss of the dark
night.

We made it out of hell and managed to survive in the underworld.

Now here we are, battle scars and all.

These scars tell the most unbelievable stories and these stories are meant
to inspire.

They are meant to give hope to those who are lost at sea,

a feeling that was always so familiar to you and me.

At Last

We passed the test with flying colours

somehow, we managed to climb out of the bottomless pit of hell and
live to tell the tale.

You and I are eternally connected

we mirror one another so effortlessly and our hearts beat in sync.

Our lives have the most uncanny similarities

we really could not make this up if we tried

it is all so divine.

There is truly nothing left to do now, nothing to do but be.

Focus on love and continue to uphold the sanctity of the Divine Union
in all that you do.

I promise

I will always meet you there.

Butterfly

Let's go into outer space, i'm ready to fly.

I was afraid before but it's finally time to test out these pretty wings of mine.

I spent so many nights trying to make sense of this thing called life,

analysing every decision I had made. How tedious.

In the dark corridor of my mind, there was always so much noise

too many tabs open at once, it felt like my brain was on fire.

The volume was so loud that I could barely function,

obsessing over what I should be doing

wondering where I should be going.

But all along, all I needed to do was just be. This was more than enough.

I had to approach this next stage radically, I had to jump over the edge fearlessly if I wanted to be free.

Acceptance was the key to my freedom. Once I accepted my divine destiny, I was finally able to be me. I delved deep within myself and found the courage to walk the path that was meant for me.

I was reborn. I was free.

No longer tormented by my own thoughts,

it was time for my wings to lead me safely into the sky.

It was finally my time to soar, my time to fly.

Love in the Sky

As I float around like a butterfly in this elaborate hologram, I can't help but wonder what else is out there.

What else is there to discover?

What secrets am I yet to uncover?

The Lovers unite in the sky and the moment they first meet, is always divine.

Keep flying north, i'll meet you there beloved.

We agreed to meet one another on Earth and nothing has changed,

you are working diligently on your souls mission, as am I.

And we must trust that when the time is right, we shall reunite and continue to fly high. Side by side.

Waiting is not an issue, it never has been

because when you know what is coming to you, you become ever so patient.

The waiting game becomes fun,

an abundance of joy comes from knowing that there is so much to look forward to.

What is truly meant for you, will never pass you by. And I know in my heart that as soon as we lock eyes, we will instantly recognise one another.

Your heart will feel that gravitational pull towards mine and words simply won't be necessary, the energy will speak for itself.

Wonderland

Undress my mind, dissect my soul

tell me, how deep are you willing to go?

Take a moment and be still, collect your thoughts

you are about to fall into the portal of the great unknown.

I promise, wonderland is truly the most magical place you will ever go.

There is so much to see, so much to know

but you have to trust the process and let everything flow.

Let go of the need to know the details,

simply open your mind and dance with me in the eternal now.

40,000 Feet

Am I on a plane or am I wherever I think I am?

It seems that I am everywhere and nowhere simultaneously.

It has become very clear to me that the mind dictates what the eyes see.

Wherever the mind goes, the body follows.

I recollect my thoughts and gaze out of the window, observing the
perfect blue sky - scattered with fluffy white clouds.

Suddenly I realise, everything is taking place in this now moment.

What is this place? Where did I go?

I ground myself into my body and relax into my heart-space.

My external reality is effortlessly merging into one divine source.

One love. One light. One sacred, everlasting soul.

There is no separation. Everything that I see, is a reflection of me and
my perception shapes my reality.

All I see is me, all I see is beauty.

There Is No Separation

As I inhale and exhale deeply, I begin to breathe in sync with the heartbeat of the Earth.

I have become one with my heart and soul, I am reconnecting with my true essence.

I close my eyes and keep my composure as I continue to breathe slowly.

I begin to see colours, patterns and numbers

so many different pieces of the divine code, the cosmic blueprint.

At long last, I am remembering

I am on my way home and my heart is the GPS.

Suddenly, the floor beneath me collapses and I fall into a bottomless pit of darkness.

My skin begins to shed like the sacred serpent

and as I touch my skinless body, I shatter into a million pieces.

I quickly adjust the camera view and become the observer

I am in awe as I look around at this beautiful, divine explosion.

The beautiful explosion that is me.

The perfect reminder that I am not this body.

Avatar

My body is simply the vessel

a vehicle that enables me to navigate this physical plane.

How blessed I am to be able to witness this once in a lifetime event, here on Earth.

I see aspects of myself as I look up at the night sky

and this divine clarity has shown me that my eternal essence will never die.

I see it now. I feel it now.

I am unravelling. I am becoming.

At last, I see that I have nothing to lose and everything to gain.

- Part Three -

Down the Rabbit Hole

Sacred Alchemy

In every passing moment, I continue to create nothing but beauty from
this chaos.

It goes on and on, like a never-ending song.

Constantly unfolding, unravelling ever so delicately

there is no beginning, there is no end

this is the divine intersection where new galaxies are born.

All roads lead back to you and the sacred inner journey.

The beautiful, often chaotic, completely hypnotic, magical journey.

How truly delightful it is, to melt so effortlessly into this.

The moments, the memories, the priceless experiences

the beautiful connections that are made between souls.

In each moment, this never-ending story continues to unfold.

To create art is to create something everlasting. Long after the soul
departs from the vessel, nothing but art remains.

The beating heart fills the canvas,

continuously unfolding.

Forever evolving.

Nothing

As I gently peeled back each layer, I came to the realisation that I was nothing.

I closed my eyes, took a deep breath and slowly collapsed into myself,

there was nothing to be found.

I came face to face with the nothingness that was me,

the nothingness that was simultaneously everything and everywhere.

I had stumbled into infinity.

In that moment, all of the old stories began to fade away,

I was no longer trying to frantically cling onto the illusion.

I was the silent witness.

Watching the movie unravel, right before my eyes. Sinking deeper into the awareness of everything that I had created.

Every projection, every story - none of it was a reflection of the real me.

They were merely stories that belonged to my character. My avatar.

The holographic manifestation of the physical aspect of me.

But none of it was real.

It was a creation of my own imagination,

something that was divinely orchestrated to help me heal.

Untitled

It is so much easier to express myself through poetry.

This inner realm of mine can be such an intense ocean

the raging waves come and go

but somehow I manage to stay afloat.

Intense highs, intense lows

nothing is ever constant.

Another day, another change.

Another wave, another fire that cannot be contained.

I Know

I know I need to stop comparing myself to others

I know I need to learn to embrace my unique beauty

I know I need to acknowledge my efforts more

I know I need to be less critical of myself

I know things are usually never as bad as I make them seem

I know there is a reason for every one of these seasons

I know life is all about perspective

I know that no one ever really dies

I know that everything in my life has been divinely orchestrated

I know I need to be less judgemental of myself

I know that I am always exactly where I need to be

I know I need to let go and trust what is unfolding

I know this path has been tailor made just for me

I know everything in my life is unfolding perfectly.

The Backdrop

The dance between The Lovers is the backdrop to all of creation

forever bonded by their devotion to one another,

bonded by their devotion to the divine.

They compliment one another perfectly

there is no one else for Her and no one else for Him.

Perfect dance partners that always move in sync. Breathe in sync. Feel in sync.

All He sees is Her and all She sees is Him.

All roads lead back to this divine dance

all roads lead back to the Divine Union

just close your eyes and be still

in this quiet place, you can feel The Lovers in your heart-space

this is where they reside

dancing through the cosmos as they gracefully kiss the sky.

Questioning Everything

Are there even any words for this?

I sit here questioning everything i've ever known and I can't help but wonder why this existence was one that my soul chose.

What is my purpose?

What does this all mean?

What is it all about?

So tired of disappointment,

tired of losing. Tired of feeling unworthy.

I find myself constantly trying to keep the mental chatter in check

desperately trying to stop myself from spiralling out of control.

Controlled chaos feels much more bearable, easier to handle

but there are times when that feeling of heaviness seems to overpower me.

And this is inevitably followed by that feeling of shame.

Shame for feeling weak

shame for feeling meek

there goes that internal chatter again, desperately trying to take centre stage.

That internal chatterbox feels like the ultimate threat

a threat to all that I have created

a threat to my mental wellbeing

a threat to the reality that I have created for myself.

I've always been an over-thinker but there are times when I seem to go so deep into my own mind, that I forget who I am. Forget where I am. Forget what I am doing.

It's as though I am in the darkest attic, clearing away cobwebs. Finding photographs and other souvenirs from the past

time-travelling to distant locations that have yet to be discovered.

This is truly a unique rollercoaster ride. Part of me wants it to end but another part of me wants to go even deeper.

Deeper into my own mind, until I find the answers that I seek.

I don't want to stop.

I can't stop

I won't stop

i've come too far to back down

time to go deeper into this rabbit hole.

Beautiful Alien

I have always found myself drawn to people who are different.

Those who are seen as 'weird'

the misunderstood souls, who spent so many lifetimes searching for a place to call home.

Of course I gravitated towards these uniquely beautiful individuals

it makes the most perfect sense. I could see myself in them, so naturally those connections always felt like home.

How exhausting it was, trying to fit into spaces that simply did not resonate.

With authenticity there is no force, it's just natural. It flows.

So here I am, no longer hoping or trying to be understood, just simply being. Trusting my intuition, as I continue to surrender to this path of deep inner healing.

In every passing moment, I can feel my strength increasing with every shadow that I slay.

At last, I see that there is no need to dilute the magical being that is me.

To be different, is beautiful.

To be beautiful, is to be you.

Riding the Wave

There is a reason for every single one of these seasons

I find myself sinking deeper into this understanding as the storm rages on.

Everything that has taken place, is a perfect example of divine orchestration

I know that there is a higher purpose to all of this.

My soul knows it. My soul specifically chose this.

The synchronicity is no coincidence, it simply cannot be.

Every test, every lesson. All blessings.

All in service of my highest good.

I look over the edge of the cliff and contemplate the idea of ending it all

but like clouds, these fleeting thoughts come and go

they are merely passers by.

Visiting for a brief moment, before they pack up their belongings and go.

The Hermit

I have never been afraid of the dark. I am always hungry for more of this delicious alchemy.

There is so much beauty in transformation. So much beauty to be found in death. So many golden keys are hidden deep within the mess.

I am slowly becoming a master of my own mind. I feel it, I believe it, I can see it.

Spending copious amounts of time alone, allows one to explore the deepest aspects of the eternal soul.

Solitude is like fertile soil. It is the perfect condition for growth.

To shine light on the darkness, is to illuminate the neglected aspects of the soul.

I feel so at home when I am bathing in the deep ocean that holds my most intimate thoughts.

What a delightful feeling it is to drown in this alchemy. In this moment, I am sinking further into the abyss and loving every second of it.

The more time I spend alone, the more I feel compelled to grow. I always seem to build so much strength when I am alone.

The true definition of a cosmic warrior.

I wonder how deep this rabbit hole goes?

22:22

Peeling back the layers like an onion.

It stings but it's a sweet kind of pain

the kind you feel when you get a tattoo.

Once again, I am hungry for more

hungry to delve into the deepest layers of my soul.

Intrigued by what I will find next

but it feels like I am in too deep,

I am drowning in my own love but I have no intention of leaving this delightful abyss.

I have come too far to back down,

I chose this path.

This path is perfect for me.

The supreme self within holds all of the keys needed to unlock every door

keys that will liberate my being and unshackle my soul.

That person I have been searching for and missing so terribly, was me.

The one I was looking for was always in my heart, sleeping peacefully.

What if?

What if this is all divinely orchestrated?

What if our entire existence is fated?

What if I had to go through those times of deep despair, so that I could come to the realisation that I do deserve to be here.

What if I had to go through those periods of wanting to die, so that I could transmute the pain and remember that I am truly divine.

What if my soul chose to experience so much death, loss and despair because I have the ability to transform after these events and see the good in every nightmare.

What if this is all just a hologram? An elaborate creation of my own imagination.

What if this is all a dream?

What if things aren't as complicated as they seem?

What if anything is possible?

What if I really am unstoppable?

What if my greatest gift, resides deep within the pain?

What if I have nothing to lose and everything to gain?

What if I thought the darkness was too frightening?

What if my ego and my soul were still fighting?

What if I thought these waves were too hard to ride?

What if I simply gave up and never tried?

What if life really does begin, once you leave the comfort zone behind?

Experiencing Bliss in the Abyss

One day, the most magical thing of all happened

I fell madly and deeply in love with me,

it was as though my vision was no longer blurry

at last, I could see.

I had melted into the deepest surrender

and I was able to witness my own divinity.

I gazed in the mirror and found myself face to face with cosmic royalty.

- Part Four -

The Purge

Time to Fly

I close my eyes and take a deep breath

the winds of change begin to gently tickle my body,

freedom is on the horizon.

I can feel it

I can taste it

I just need to close my eyes and jump.

My mind can be so easily deceived by the illusion of fear

but my heart is filled with the strength and courage of a Lion.

I know I can do this. It all begins and ends in the mind.

It is time to jump into the great unknown and leave my comfort zone behind.

I see so much more with my eyes closed.

When I close my eyes, I can feel.

When I close my eyes, I see what is real.

The Test

How many times will I repeat the same lesson before I finally learn?

I know the answers but it seems that my head and my heart are not in alignment

these eyes have been deceiving me

and in this moment, my heart feels ineffectual and weak.

But regardless of this, I know that there is no shame in failing a test. The more I fail, the better I get.

This is the perfect opportunity to master my craft

because after all, everything is art.

The more I continue to repeat the test, the more I am able to see.

I find myself experiencing the same lesson from different perspectives and this is good because it enhances my senses.

There is no way that this has all happened by chance,

every part of the movie plays out exactly as it is supposed to.

Each path that I take, leads me back to myself. Every road leads me back home.

Some routes may take longer than others but the destination always remains the same.

Self-mastery is the key. Self-Mastery is the purpose of this divine journey.

The Love Within

All she wanted was love

all she wanted, was to find someone that she could trust.

Someone to have and to hold,

yet she went on searching aimlessly in the wilderness

a deer among a pack of wolves.

But this love was never going to be found in another

to find this love, she had to dig deep. She had to go within. She had to go beyond the surface, to the elusive space beneath the skin.

She had to lose herself at sea,

she had to sink deep into the ocean and rediscover her divinity.

But this was never going to be an easy task.

Until the mission was complete, nothing else would fall into place

this was the most crucial piece of the puzzle.

She had to find the love within,

she had to surrender to the Divine Union between Her and Him.

Stay

You tell me you want me to stay

but all I want to do is fly away.

These delicate wings give me the freedom that I so desperately crave.

I need freedom and space to fly, this is non-negotiable.

I need freedom to float like a graceful butterfly.

Perhaps I am afraid that attachment will hold me back, so a part of me is afraid to vocalise how I truly feel.

If I get lost in you, what will happen to me?

Beloved, are you able to love me and let me be free? Because I refuse to be your Persephone

I cannot be one of your possessions

if my life becomes all about you, where does that leave me?

What about my hopes? What about my dreams?

Right now, all I want to do is fly high and step into my destiny

I love you but you and I both know that we were never meant to be.

We each have our own path to follow. Our own destiny. Our own Dharma.

So fly pretty bird, spread your wings and touch the sky.

So Much Space

It was so quiet the day you left

suddenly there was so much space.

Miles and miles of empty space

stretching far beyond my teary eyes could see.

I became a hollow bamboo,

I was nothing but a blank canvas.

But those salty, sorrow filled tears became tears of joy

because when you are nothing, you can become anything.

It was time for me to see what I would evolve into without you.

Time to make the most of all of this empty space,

there is no longer any room to play it safe.

Thank You for the Lessons

You never deserved this precious love of mine

but I was too nice and my boundaries were weak

I wanted to save you.

There I was, foolishly hoping I could change you

but what right did I have to interfere with your journey?

We were both using one another, deep down.

You took my kindness for weakness

meanwhile, I wanted to mould you into somebody else

someone that I could truly see myself being with.

But of course, I failed. Miserably.

You showed me who you were from the start

but I continued to ignore all of the red flags,

I guess it was the empath in me.

You know what they say:

the empath attracts the narcissist

and you my love, showed up right on time.

You were the mirror that I needed to see.

A mirror that I had seen so many times before

a mirror that I clearly needed more time to explore

but in an an effort to run away from myself, I ran straight into you

and ended up running into myself, again.

This was the great turning point.

Something was different this time, something had changed.

I had finally opened my eyes

I was able to see through your very elaborate disguise.

So thank you for the lessons

you showing up as yourself, was truly a blessing.

Thank you for showing me how much I was settling.

- Part 5 -

Metamorphosis

The Art of Dying

My most recent death was a particularly profound one

I felt so much beautiful pain pulsating through my veins.

As the energy made its way to my third eye, the pain transformed into a blinding beacon of light. Creating the most magical explosion of deep, inner knowing.

I was reborn. I was brand new.

I had transformed into another version of myself.

What timeline had I accidentally jumped into?

Suddenly, nothing made sense

but simultaneously - in that timeless moment, everything made sense.

I was everywhere and nowhere

I was everything and nothing.

Complete and utter peace and tranquility washed over me and drenched every cell in my entire body.

Every, single part of me felt hydrated and rejuvenated.

Chaos

Let me tell you a little something about the dark night

it crept up on me and completely took me by surprise

I didn't expect to be stripped down to my core like this.

I feel naked. Exposed.

Completely vulnerable and out in the open,

there is no longer anywhere to hide.

This heaviness is a feeling like no other,

it was like the entire house collapsed on top of me.

Everything collapsed and fell to the ground

all I could see was chaos. Carnage.

How do I fix this? Where do I begin?

Is it possible to save anything?

How does one go about cleaning up a mess of this magnitude?

Then suddenly, the answers came.

A flash of fresh insight washed over me.

The only way out of this, was to sink deep into the chaos and bathe in it

be at one with it and see the divine order in it.

Observe it. Understand it. Transmute it.

Time to Tell a New Story

Release all fear and live courageously from the heart

there is no longer a need to cling onto those old stories of the past.

It is time to tell a new story, the story that you wish to bring to fruition.

Tell the story that most resonates with your soul,

then sit back and watch the magic unfold.

Start deliberately co-creating with source,

start deliberately creating with yourself.

There is no need to take a backseat,

this is your life. So return to the driver's seat.

This is your movie, you are the director

so direct your movie and make it as magnificent as can be.

Because there is nothing that you cannot achieve

just think big, have faith and believe.

Mirror Meditation

The past feels like a distant memory

a figment of my imagination, an elaborate creation.

Looking in the mirror is an out of body experience.

Who is this person I see before me?

It's true, I really am not this body.

I see my aura, I see my core essence, I see my heart and soul

I see my inner child, I see my inner smile

I see a caterpillar that has morphed into a butterfly

I see a sweet, delicate flower blooming

I see an angelic beam of light

I see a Goddess with the fierce spirit of a warrior.

I see energy

I see divinity

I see all that is me.

Meet Me Here, in the Eternal Now

Meet me here, in the eternal now and just let everything unfold naturally. There is no need to force, just flow.

There is nothing else to do now but take off the mask and show the world the real you.

Attending this party as yourself is more than enough

because this is all about the Divine Union between you and you.

You are cosmically connected to everything around you and there is no separation. There never has been.

Nothing but love surrounds you and there is no external enemy. There never has been, these are just stories.

There are no obstacles.

Everything is rigged in your favour and the universe is constantly working with you, to bring you whatever it is that you desire.

You only need to align yourself with whatever you wish to bring to fruition.

How truly magical the universe is

and as a cosmic creation of source, you are a part of this.

The entire universe resides within you and every passing moment is another opportunity to create your very own masterpiece.

Do you see the magic?

Can you feel it flowing through your veins?

As the Divine Creator and the most gifted painter, you can create anything. The canvas is blank.

You have all of the tools you need to create a one of a kind masterpiece.

So I dare you to dive into the timeline of your dreams.

Commitment Issues

How could I commit to you, when I couldn't even commit to myself?

I neglected my own needs, hopes, wishes and dreams

I failed to see my divinity and I settled for less than I truly deserved,

time and time again.

I was running away from myself. Running at full speed.

Running from my power

running from my gifts

running from my problems

running from my dreams.

But at some point, I grew tired of playing that game

it was time to stop running. It was time to face myself.

Time to take accountability for the mess that I had orchestrated.

Time to face the music,

time to admit that I hadn't treated myself in the way that I should have.

Time to forgive myself.

Time to start again and create a new beginning.

Time to tell a brand new story.

Time to commit, to me.

Point of Awareness

This beautiful path of mine, perfectly crafted so long ago.

My soul knew exactly what it wanted to learn from this human experience.

Although sometimes I feel so tired, I know that divine order is always at play.

I have the inner knowing that this is all just a game.

This is what has kept my inner flame shining bright, during the darkest, coldest nights.

Shakti requires total surrender.

She requires total devotion once you enter Her mysterious chamber of secrets.

But upon entering her lair, you feel nothing but an overwhelming feeling of perfect love.

She emanates a love so deep that it collapses into itself and creates the most magical explosion of total bliss.

As I continue to walk this unpaved path, I am extremely grateful for all that I am and all of the work that has been done. The work that continues to be done. Day in, day out.

There is truly no end to this, it goes on and on.

So what else is there to do but dance to this delightful song?

Truly thankful for every passing moment that I am able to continue this divine dance.

Always evolving, constantly unfolding.

Metamorphosis.

The Party

Don't you know that every moment of your existence is a special occasion?

Life itself is a celebration and you are the guest of honour.

Every single moment is divine in so many ways

there is so much gratitude to be felt

so much love for everything that has taken place.

How beautiful it is to dive into these moments and completely immerse myself in them.

I see nothing but magic in the air

everything within the cosmos is dancing, all that I need is right here.

This precious life of mine, is truly a priceless gift

there really are no words for this.

Dark Nights of the Soul

I spent so much time locked away in my room, just staring at the ceiling

feeling hopeless, scared and confused about my entire existence.

Praying somebody would come and save me,

knowing nobody would because nobody could.

I had to save myself.

But in order to save myself, I had to love myself

I had to believe I was worthy of being saved.

I was screaming at the top of my lungs but somehow, nobody seemed to hear me.

Nobody seemed to notice that I was standing at the edge of a cliff.

How was this possible?

I found myself suspended between worlds

I had stumbled into the wilderness.

With every breath that I took, I could feel my connection to everything around me slipping away.

I was drowning in an ocean of my own sorrow.

I would often dread the idea of waking up the next day and experiencing this thing called life all over again.

While simultaneously feeling guilty for my apparent lack of appreciation for life.

What was wrong with me?

So much confusion, conflicted feelings and inner turmoil,

All I could do was ride the wave and wait for the storm to pass.

The Divine Union

Look at you, a true masterpiece. So divine, so supreme.

You deserve nothing but the best and there are no limitations to what you can manifest.

Tell me, what do you believe?

What runs through your subconscious as you breathe?

Divine cosmic being, don't you know that you possess all of the love that you are so desperately seeking?

Can't you see that there's a divine order to these people that you keep meeting?

The universe is always talking but how can you hear, if you are aways speaking?

Close your eyes, be still and go within.

There's buried treasure waiting to be found, deep beneath the skin.

Peel back the layers and prepare for the Divine Union between Her and Him.

Don't you know that you are your own twin?

Fan the flames.

There's no need to look outside of yourself, this love can be found within.

Look at the blessing in the reflection.

Look at and bless your reflection.

You see, everything has a divine connection

It just requires closer inspection.

Clarity

When you shine love into the darkest of corners, you begin to see that everything is the most perfect reflection of you.

Everything has its own sacred connection to you

all roads lead back to you.

So let love be the beacon of light that will safely guide you through this dark night.

Love is the most potent healing potion.

Love is always there, it never quits.

Free from judgement,

love just is.

- Part 6 -

Phoenix Rising

Returning to Source

It was in me all along

I always had the tools in my possession

but I had to remember who I was first.

I had to remember what I already had, before I could make use of it.

If you don't know what you have, how can you use it?

The darkness was always going to be the perfect environment for my
growth.

Seeds grow in dark soil

they take their time and grow upwards, as they are nourished and given
sunlight.

Nature always takes its time

yet somehow, everything gets done.

Continue to shine light into the darkness

pour love into it and watch it transform into something new. Something
astonishing.

Because sometimes, the most beautiful beings grow in the darkest places.

Dark, quiet, secluded spaces where it's just you and you.

The Reunion

Why do you think of yourself as a mere mortal?

Combat the enemy within

reignite the fire, harmonise the energy between Her and Him

dive into the ocean and explore the abyss.

Deep within the ocean lies the potion. That's the twist.

Bathe in the chaos, then transmute the energy,

there's an art to it

but once you master it, that feeling right there is heavenly.

Go with the flow and eventually you will float,

surrender is the key.

Turn down the volume and drown out the background noise

these codes are right under your nose,

hidden in plain sight.

Everyone that you meet has a piece of the code.

Dissect and extract the messages that need to be known

and make use of the time that you spend alone.

The dark night of the soul is the initiation,

it shows you that this game is all your own elaborate creation.

The Art of Play

Every deliciously, divine moment is filled with play.

There is no separation between work and play. There is only play.

Miles and miles of endless opportunities to engage in this lost art.

The world is a playground that stretches far beyond the eyes can see

and in every passing moment, more is being revealed.

Because contrary to how it may seem, nothing is concealed

everything is right here, right now.

It all exists simultaneously, vibrating at different frequencies.

So what station are you tuned into?

This will always determine what you see.

The art of fine tuning ones dial is a delicate process.

A process that requires patience and perseverance.

A process that cannot be rushed.

A process that unfolds slowly.

One breath at a time. One step at a time. One moment at a time.

The Moment It All Changed

All of the pain that I endured was not in vain.

This whole time, I have been an alchemist in training.

I managed to transform these beautiful battle scars into the most spectacular wings

what a beautiful feeling it is, to make peace with the past.

At last, I am no longer wearing a mask

no longer ashamed to tell my story

no longer afraid to stand up and shine bright,

rightfully claiming what is mine.

This is my time.

I see the divine order in every part of my journey

everything that takes place in one moment, is preparation for what is to come next.

The universe always delivers what is needed, at the perfect time

and like a spider's web, this creation of mine has been so intricately spun.

Crafted with love, every single detail so carefully thought out

every aspect pre-planned, long before my arrival here on Earth.

So much love and care went into this masterpiece

As I sit here writing this, all I can do is gently exhale and melt into a state of ecstatic bliss.

No matter what is going on around me, everything is perfect.

The eternal witness that lies within my beating heart, shall never come to any harm.

The divine essence that dances within the physical vessel is immortal, untouchable

it goes on and on, existing. Being. Breathing.

There really is no end to this,

this human experience is like a painting that never seems to be complete

there is always more to paint, always something else to create

and of course, every instrument belongs in this great symphony

absolutely nothing is ever out of place.

Welcome to the divine intersection where poetry collides with live art and creates an explosion of magical music.

Music is life and this life is a musical

truly the greatest composition of all time.

Cosmic Whisper

Purely authentic, sweet and angelic,

the eyes never lie

and the heart sings the sweetest melody every time it beats.

Constantly surrendering to love,

making nothing but fine art in every passing moment.

This is the definition of poetry.

Poetry is life itself

poetry is love

poetry is art

poetry cannot be rushed.

To create poetry, is to create fine art.

To create poetry, is to create a masterpiece.

An eternal piece of the heart, that will forever last.

Fated

How amazing it is, to no longer be waist deep in the abyss.

For so long, I have dreamt of this.

I screamed for this, I spent so many nights hoping there would be a
sudden end to this.

Because when I was lost in the darkness, all I knew was unhappiness.

But as hard as it was, I managed to remain hopeful that there would be a
plot twist. A shocking turn of events.

Something to restore my faith in me,

something that would restore my faith in humanity.

I was so desperate for a sign, any sign.

A signal from above, that would show me explicitly that I was still loved.

Because once I had my awakening, anything surface level was simply not
enough.

So as I write this, it feels as though a heavy weight has been lifted, I feel
like I have been gifted.

Gifted with another chance to live.

It simply cannot be a coincidence that I managed to make it out of the
abyss,

this feels fated.

A love letter from Her to Him

Thinking of you, sends me into a deep meditative state

all I want to do is express my love in the form of poetry, as we continue to create.

You are a dream come true

you are everything that I have been manifesting and so much more.

You are a precious, rare being that I truly adore

and you have exceeded all of my expectations, in every way possible.

I feel so blessed to be in the presence of such greatness.

The beauty of your soul, truly takes my breath away

and when I look into your eyes, I see an angel.

I see someone who has been hurt many times before

yet somehow, still manages to remain kind with intentions that are so pure.

I see a sweet soul, with a heart that is soft and full of love

oh what a special gift from the cosmos you are.

You travelled across many galaxies to be here

and for that, I am grateful.

A true cosmic traveller, who never seems to get tired of shifting between dimensions.

All of those selfless acts of kindness

I promise you, they never go unnoticed.

Your beauty lights up the darkest room

and you only seem to get more beautiful, as you continue to bloom.

So this poem is dedicated to you, my love.

Thank you for never leaving my side.

Thank you for continuously making me feel inspired.

Thank you for never hardening your heart.

Thank you for simply showing up as you.

Thank you for continuing to speak your truth,

you are my inspiration. The perfect role model.

You are all that I aspire to be,

you are the most perfect reflection of me.

So this poem is my gift to you.

Unwrap it slowly.

Dance With Me

To truly see me, is to love me

to meet me where I am, is to dance with me

to show up to the party as yourself,

is to reflect the raw authenticity and divinity that resides within me.

Because you and I are poetry

so just continue to flow with me

as we add more pages to this beautiful book of poetry.

Sweet Solitude

This time spent in solitude feels very deliberate,

it feels divinely orchestrated

but much of it is beyond my comprehension.

Countless months spent wrapped up in my cosy cocoon,

just waiting.

Waiting until it was time to reemerge as a beautiful butterfly,

ready to ascend to great heights and fly.

A Toast to Life

This sweet, precious heart of mine has truly stood the test of time.

Sailed through every initiation, with grace and patience.

Even though the weather was often stormy

and my vision was sometimes clouded with fog,

I was always able to feel my way through.

This intuition of mine never failed me, it was always there

regardless of how many times I ignored it,

it always showed up and never turned its back on me.

Always in the background, leading me in the right direction.

It held my hand, ever so softly

and reassured me that all would be well, if I continued to trust and have faith.

It whispered words of encouragement into my ears and wrapped a blanket of love around me.

This is the unconditional love that the universe exudes

this is the love that resides within you and it is utterly pure and true.

So in this eternal moment, I am grateful.

Grateful for the strength of my ancestors that runs through my veins

grateful to have the most magical tools at my disposal,

tools that my soul knew I would be able utilise.

Grateful for every test that I managed to pass.

Grateful for the mistakes that led me to this place of clarity,

clarity that I so desperately longed and prayed for.

Clarity that eluded me for so long

but I had to learn the art of surrender first

I had to learn to release attachment to a fixed outcome.

It was paramount that I was able to let go and trust what was coming,

even when I wasn't always entirely sure of what was on the horizon.

But none of that mattered anymore because I was home.

I had returned home to myself in the most beautiful way,

I felt safe within my own being.

Safe in my own skin.

Scorpio Rising

I seem to find myself in a constant trance

walking through the wilderness, searching for a place to call home.

It truly devastated my soul, when I realised that I had never felt at home
anywhere before.

These eyes of mine have seen so many beautiful places

yet I still find myself searching for something that has no face or name.

My mind cannot fully conceive what it is

I have no idea what it looks like

but there is a deep inner knowing within my heart,

a knowing that constantly reassures me that there is a home for me.
Somewhere.

But before this can be found, felt and recognised

I must first feel at home within myself.

Of course, this is easier said than done

particularly for someone like me.

Someone who never quite fit in anywhere.

I found myself constantly drifting between realms

weaving in and out of different dimensions.

The lens through which I see the world is truly unique

and my path is radically unconventional.

There is no blueprint for me to follow,

no one that can be used as a guide.

Whenever I tried to follow what I had seen before,

I hit a brick wall, every time.

'That's what you get for following the crowd' said the universe.

'Are you ready to follow the calling of your own heart now?'

Are you ready to create the reality that most resonates with your soul?

Are you ready to be the real you?

These questions danced around my mind persistently

like dragonflies on a dark starry night.

At some point, it got so loud that I could no longer ignore it.

I could no longer ignore the call to come home to myself

I desperately wanted to get off this rollercoaster ride and return to the peaceful lake that I once knew,

my sacred sanctuary. The purest, deepest essence that resides within me.

The untainted aspect of me

the sacred space within, that can never be disturbed.

That which cannot be seen or heard.

A Heart to Heart With My Inner Child

Tell me your dreams little one

look up at Luna and make a wish.

All of these dreams of yours are destined to come true,

I promise you.

All you ever have to do, is be you. Without any filter.

Raw, unprocessed and natural

Surrender to me, i've got you

I am your protector

and when you speak, you will always be heard.

It is safe to be you,

it is safe to let your tender heart sing.

Tell me, what it is you want to do.

What do you wish to create?

I promise you,

I will always provide a safe space for you to express yourself and embrace your magical, angelic essence.

So take my hand sweet soul

and together we will fulfil our divine, cosmic plan.

Whole and Complete

Me meeting you, was all about me coming back into union with me.

A wonderful manifestation of my own creation

the true definition of divine orchestration,

all perfectly planned.

All we ever needed to do was let the movie play out,

surrender fully to the higher plan and dance together in the eternal now.

Even when no words were spoken,

you and I both knew what was taking place

we had the awareness all along.

Regardless of whether we were physically together,

we were always constantly dancing to the same cosmic song.

The Final Push

I can remember the exact moment that you were conceived.

Right away, I was excited to finally meet you in the physical realm

I dreamt about every single part of you,

right down to the last detail. It consumed me. I was obsessed.

Growing you inside of me was the biggest test of my patience

and the most remarkable way for me to demonstrate my capacity to love myself, unconditionally.

Because you are an extension of me, the most perfect reflection of me.

All I could seem to think about, was how it would feel to have you in my presence

and what my reality would be like, with you in it.

Quantum jumping and remote viewing did not suffice,

I wanted the real thing.

You were always my greatest teacher, right from the start.

You taught me that the most wonderful things are worth waiting for.

It takes time to grow something so precious and life-changing,

there is really no need to rush, when you know what's coming to you.

What's yours, is yours.

I have never heard truer words.

There is truly a process to everything

and skipping steps is completely out of the equation.

It's wild to think about how much fear plagued my mind.

Was I worthy of conceiving and receiving something so great?

What if the time came and I failed miserably?

Was I strong enough to handle so much responsibility?

Growing such a divine, pure creation of love inside of me, led me to question myself in so many ways.

But hidden deep within all of that doubt, was strength

a hidden reservoir of strength and power that I never knew existed.

Through that exhausting process of questioning myself,

I was suddenly able to smash through the illusion of fear and remember who I was, beyond the veil.

In that moment, everything changed

I remember that I was made for this. I trained for this.

For the first time, I realised all that I was capable of being.

I remembered my divinity

and instantly, my power was brought back to me.

I was ready to give birth.

I was finally ready to bring my beautiful creation to life.

Special Messages

Just when I thought this book was finished, I received guidance that I needed to add one last chapter and here it is.

Reading poetry takes you on a journey that can make you feel as though your emotions are being taken on a rollercoaster ride. Filled with many twists and turns. So I wanted to end this book on a high note and provide a space for you to come back to, whenever you need to. These messages are timeless and being a firm believer in the divine orchestration of life, I trust that the messages that are meant for you, will always find their way to you and be received at the perfect time.

If you feel guided to do so, just flip open this chapter or this book to a random page and trust that the perfect page will find you. I do this often when I read books. It is truly amazing how the words on the page, end up being the exact words that I need to read in that moment.

May this chapter give you all that it is supposed to. Simply read with an open heart and melt into that sweet state of stillness, as you read these words that have been infused with love.

My Dedication to You

Stay focused

you have a vision to bring to fruition.

You are not reading this poem by chance

and it is no coincidence that you are here on Earth right now,

your soul chose to come here.

It specifically chose this mission.

It's ok to take a nap if you get tired,

just as long as you remember who you are when you wake up

because everything about you is unique

and nobody else can do what you do, the way that you do it.

So every time you look in the mirror,

don't be fooled by what you see.

The divine essence that is you, resides deep within

it goes way deeper than the smooth surface that is the skin.

You are eternal and your soul is so valuable.

Truly beautiful, like cosmic stardust.

So honour all that you are

and above all else, remember that you can and you will go far.

Dancing in the Sky

You can soar to great heights

you can make the seemingly impossible happen,

just continue to show up and don't be afraid to shine.

Being yourself, is the most beautiful thing of all.

So I wrote this poem just for you

I have infused these words with love and I trust that they will reach you

wherever you are, whoever you are

simply open your heart and the messages will find you.

Open your mind and trust in the power of the divine.

You are never alone

and there are many loving angels floating beside you, as you walk this unpaved road.

Eternal Love

You notice so much more when you go slow and dance with the flow of the Divine Mother.

She will always tell you where to go

she never abandons you or leaves you out in the cold.

Be still and bring your gaze towards that which exists in nature,

a tree, a simple flower, the crisp texture of an autumn leaf.

Can you feel Her presence?

Can you feel Her love?

Close the curtains that are your eyelids and focus on the space behind them.

A bottomless well of love resides there, this love is within you.

This love is you, it nourishes you and never leaves you.

Like a trusted friend, it is always there

ready to cradle you in the warmest embrace.

So even though there may be times when you feel completely alone,

just know that the entire universe is dancing within you.

Be still and feel the presence of this eternal love.

Faith

Trust your own timeline, you are not behind.

Everything is unfolding in the most perfect way

and with each passing day, you are making progress.

Just be gentle with yourself as you ride each wave

and remember that everything changes, once you shift the perspective of your gaze.

Surrender and have faith. You are protected, sweet soul

you are here on Earth because you have an important role to play.

There is nobody else who can do what you do.

There is nobody else like you.

You are a rare diamond, constantly shining,

even in those moments when you cannot see your divinity.

May your heart be filled with perfect peace, as you read these words

and may you always remember that you are the most perfect reflection of the most high.

- Notes from me to you -

Dear Sweet Soul,

Can you see how beautiful you are?

You, are a masterpiece.

YOU, are the master piece.

A one of a kind painting, there is no other like you.

Take a look in the mirror and admire the magnificent being that is staring back at you.

Love,

Ayesha

Dearest You,

I know sometimes life gets tough,

I know sometimes it feels like all hope is lost

but you are doing amazing.

You have endured so much and here you are, standing strong.

Be proud of yourself. Be proud of all that you are and all that you are yet to be.

Just wait and see, you will get your time in the sun.

Like the sacred phoenix, you shall rise and shine bright.

Just keep your faith strong, have patience and enjoy the beautiful journey that you are on.

Love,

Ayesha

Beloved,

Those dark nights may come knocking at the door but they will not last forever, nothing does.

Remember this, the next time you feel like all hope is lost.

Every single wave that life asks you to ride, is perfect for you.

You were made for this. You've got this and I believe in you.

Some days will feel like total bliss and others will feel like you are trapped in an overwhelming blanket of hopelessness.

But you will make it through.

Lean in and use this as an opportunity to go deeper within.

All my love,

Ayesha

Dearest soul,

Always remember that you are beautiful and the entire universe resides within you.

To be you, is to be beautiful. To be beautiful is to be the angelic soul that is you.

All my love,

Ayesha

Dearest Earthling,

All you ever needed to be was yourself.

Isn't that the most beautiful thing of all?

Love,

Ayesha.

Dear Beloved Soul,

Take a deep breath and bring your awareness to your body.

Can you feel the magic in the sweet space in between each breath that you take?

In this eternal moment, there is nothing to do but be.

Just breathe, slow and steady. Rest in this deep meditative state.

This energy is all you. This energy is yours. Bask in your divinity.

All my love,

Ayesha

Dear You,

You, are so beautiful. Truly.

Forget about those who failed to see you in your entirety.

Your soul is much too grand to play small,
so stand up tall and just be you. Whatever that looks like, sweet jewel.

Forget about everyone who tried to extinguish your violet flame.

A wild, electric, unique soul like yours simply cannot be tamed.

So be wild. Be like a playful child.

Be free and embody all of your sacred divinity!

Inhale deeply and as you exhale, close your eyes and melt into the
totality of infinity.

Love,

Ayesha

Dear Sweet Soul,

*There may be times when you feel completely alone
but I want you to know that you are supported.
The universe supports you.*

Please never forget this.

*Go outside and let your inner child bathe in the magnificence of the
effortless beauty of nature.*

Gaze at the trees, they are your reflection.

*Listen to the birds as they sing their sweet song, admire the perfect
petals of a delicate Rose.*

*All around, reminders of your divinity can be found.
Mother Nature is constantly whispering words of wisdom and
encouragement to you.*

Let the Divine Mother cradle you gently in her warm embrace.

Love,

Ayesha

Dear Divine Cosmic Being,

Just as The Moon waxes and wanes, as it goes though its various phases - so do you.

Some cycles ask you to dive into the darkness of your own inner ashram and quietly be at one with yourself.
Other cycles invite you to take centre stage and sing courageously from the heart.

Some cycles are very quiet and slow. This time period is calling you to just be where you are, calling you to be still.

The universe is not punishing you. Where you are, is where you need to be.

Golden nuggets of information lie within this sacred vicinity, just close your eyes and tune into the magic.

Infinite love,

Ayesha

Dear You,

Look how far you have come!

What a long road it has been. There have been many trials and tribulations, so many tears. You have managed to face so many of your fears. How courageous you are.

You, my dear - are truly spectacular in every way.

So in this moment, I just want to say that I appreciate you and all that you do.

This is a joint mission and we are all working together.

This love that we share, has the ability to create new worlds.

This love cannot be contained. This is the greatest love of all, truly the most magnificent gift to us all.

Love always,

Ayesha

Dear Magical Being,

I promise, there is a divine order to all that you are seeing.

This is all a part of the creators perfect plan. There may be so much that you cannot yet see but all will be revealed, when it needs to be.

Just close your eyes and believe.

Feel the magic that dances so gracefully in the air. Come into your body and know that you deserve to be here. You are needed here on Earth.

You are such a sacred and precious piece of this expansive, cosmic puzzle.

Keep going, keep growing, keep shining. You are a diamond.

Sending you love,

Ayesha

Dear You,

Be present in the moment and you will feel the presence of the moment.

There are so many wonderful presents hidden within every, tender moment.

Close your eyes, breathe deep and feel the magic that is running through your veins.

Envision the night sky, scattered with stars and remember that this is a perfect reflection of all that you are.

You are a star. A radiant ball of light, shining bright.

Each moment, is another opportunity to see the true essence of what you are.

Every step that you take, brings you closer to remembering your innate ability to thrive and glide gracefully across the night sky, like a shooting star.

All that you need is right here, there are no limits to how high you can fly.

Believe in yourself and embrace every scar that has made you who you are.

You are divinity in the flesh.

Love,

Ayesha

Dear you,

There is no hurry to get to your destination because you have already arrived.

From the moment your Mother gave birth to you, you have been in alignment with the flow of the celestial tides.

The only place to be, is right here.

Rest in this space and know that there is no hurry to get anywhere.

You are always on time.

Love always,

Ayesha

ABOUT THE AUTHOR

Living moment to moment, Ayesha Grant embodies the essence of poetry in all that she does.

Like a true mystic, she simply surrenders to each moment that presents itself and lets love lead the way. Trusting that everything will always unfold exactly as it needs to.

Seeing every event as a divinely orchestrated piece of the cosmic puzzle, which serves as a valuable contribution to the greater whole. From the perspective of her own unique lens, every experience is another instrument to add to the magnificent orchestra that is life.

Currently residing somewhere in the wilderness.

CONTACT

SOCIAL MEDIA:

TWITTER: @DANCINGHERENOW

INSTAGRAM: @AYSHGRANT

Printed in Great Britain
by Amazon

24157173R00081